Tears of Love

—

Tears of Loss

Tears of Love

—

Tears of Loss

A collection of poetry by
Kelley E. Howe Nolan

Thoughts about the ups and downs of caring for someone you love.

Dedication

This collection of poetry is for
those seeking a sense of comfort.
The struggles and emotions of
caring for someone you love can
ignite feelings that are unfamiliar
and scary. These feelings are
okay to have. Life can be scary
and trying to care for a loved one
who is losing the battle is hard.
Stay in the fight — you're not
alone.

Introduction

When I first thought about putting together a collection of poems about Alzheimer's Disease, I thought someone else might relate to what we're going through. We were officially diagnosed in November 2017 by a kind and compassionate neuropsychologist. This came after being referred to by my husband's neurologist for testing. We were both astounded by the news and, as it sunk in, both Michael and I took turns trying to make each other feel somewhat better.

This book is a look back and a review of some of the poetry I wrote during that time, beginning with November 2017. I selected poems that were about this disease and its impact on me—which are really my reaction to what I see in Michael. It sounded so easy. In fact, it sounded so easy that I didn't do anything to get started for a while because I thought it would just take a little time: gather, read, sort... simple. It's been about a year and a half since I began. I finally sat down, with a glass of wine nearby, in early 2021 and began reading poems that I thought might capture my thoughts on this disease. It all came back. The tsunami of emotions. I would read a poem and know exactly what my frame of mind was at the time. Poetry is a way for me to process and express my feelings. Throughout this project I've shared poems with others that have been, or are currently, in the same position as we are. Whether it's Alzheimer's Disease, Parkinson's Disease, or Dementia, they've told me that they can relate as they too are caring for someone they love.

I hope this collection resonates in some small way, providing comfort to the struggles of the caregiver and those loved ones they hold so deeply in their hearts. Not all poems will have titles as it is hard to title something that can mean so many things to so many people.

Thank you.

— Kelley E. Howe Nolan

I never doubted my
Belief in God
I question other representatives
But I never doubted
My own choice of faith,
God has always been
Present in my mind
Prayers answered
Not always my hope
But eventually
Understood
And accepted.
Tough times behind me
Confusion presently
Hope is my future
God will be with me.

My mind
My mood
Constantly alert
Wary of your
Changes
Changes in voice
In your posture
Your eyes.

My mind
My mood
Constantly afraid
Of saying
The wrong thing
Of doing
Something wrong
Making you upset.

My mind
My moods
Are exhausted
And I'm going
To get help
So I can be
Of help.

I thought and I believed
I knew a lot
About mental health,
Mental illness
But,
Looking back
I only knew one perspective
A "job related" view

I have grown.
I read and search
I try to grow in my
Education
I need "new tools"
In my toolbox.

Mental health and mental
Health challenges
Face me every day
At home
At work
As I face the future.

It didn't take long
A few minutes on the
Phone
You hung up, turned around
And made your angry
Announcement
You shared your dismay
And a flicker of anger
Flashed through your eyes
Lit up the air surrounding us,
Like the briefest
Flash of lightning
I am not ready
Nor am I prepared to react
To a situation
On the not-too-distant
Horizon.

Royal Regency Inn

It's freezing outside
Windows covered

In frost
As we warm the

Car
And ourselves
Ready to venture into
Traffic
On an early
Morning
In a foreign town
Feeling anxious
Knowing change
Is in our future.

The awkward silence
Filling the room
As all eyes
Flick from face to face
No one making
Actual eye contact
No one daring
To speak first
No one
Seeing
Anyone.

It's been a while
My energy level low
My thoughts cloudy
Nothing comes clearly
Until now
I think of us
The future promising
Days filled with love
And the joy of
Our time together
However long that is.

For My Love

Confusion ever-present
Conversations repeated
Over and over again
Creating wonder.
Frustration,
And sadness.
Time will tell
Wounds will heal
And conversations
Will change.

Entering another chapter
My life
A never-ending novel
Complete with mystery
Adventure, laughter, love
And loss,
Each chapter closing
Yet
Leading into the next
Series of unknown
New events
Yet to come.

ALZ

Little things

"No morning coffee"
Brought to our bedside
Longer "naps"
And shorter patience
The sound of music
From decades past
Fill the house
And your mind
Recalling the days
When you "drove this"
And "went there"
But yesterday
And early this morning,
Forgotten already
The process evolving
And life crawls
Moving forward
Slowly.

My life is chaotic
Every day a kaleidoscope
Of colors
Never the same pattern
But beautiful in its depth
Of light and dark
Only to evolve into
Another day
Of chaos.

The hum of the refrigerator
The soft glow of the
Kitchen light
As a new day begins
My wanting every moment
With you
To count
As I feel days
Weeks,
Years
Are numbered
The end, sooner
Than later,
Sooner than
Expected.
Wake up,
Wake up and relish
The new day
We've been given.

Lift Your Veil

If every day
Is a new day
A new beginning
Another new opportunity
A fresh start
Then why can't I
Show you
How this works?
You have such pleasure
And joy
Ahead of you
Ahead for us, together
Why won't you
See it,
Believe it,
Live it,
In hope?

Don't Forget Me

Are you giving up
Giving in
Quitting?
Do you have
Zero hope of
A future
Together?
One filled with
Joy, blessings
And love?
Why?
Why are you giving
Up,
Giving in,
Quitting?
What can I do?
What can I say?
Don't forget me.

This is What I Hope

You stare into space
I hope you see love
You move with slowness
I hope it's because you want
To be careful
You ask repeatedly "what"
I hope it's because you want
To be clear about what you heard
You listen to song after song
I hope it's because you love music
Your sleep longer and more soundly
I hope you dream,
A lot about living.

A glance at you
From across the room
Fills my heart
And my mind
With worry
And sadness.
I see your wonder,
Your questioning look,
Do you see mine?

In the earliest of morning
When the sky is waking up
The birds begin their music
And coffee fills my cup
I think of you and smile wide
The day ahead looks warm
The ocean moans with every wave
And a brand-new day is born.

Time to let go
Move on
Move forward
Sideways
Even backward
Move without
Fear
Move with joy
Thanks
And love
Move to hope
Move towards
Another dimension
Of life
And living
With mindfulness
In my heart
In all my actions.

A new day approaches
The sunlight creating shadows
As it begins to climb
The sounds of birds, clocks
And cars
Mixing together, calming my thoughts
What will today bring?
New adventures to be tucked
Away in the back of my mind
Or "same old same old"?
As I contemplate the answer
I know it all falls to me
And the choices I will make.

Dr. Dickinson's Lobby

Waiting
Waiting and wondering
Wondering what new changes
Are ahead for us
You, me, the entire family
Will it be long
Will time slow down
So we can catch up
With life?
Or,
Will the speed of ill health
Be an example of
Today's technology,
Moving so quickly forward
That we will always
Be waiting
And wondering
About new changes.

To The Man Inside The Man

You are a loving
Caring and gentle man
Who sings loudly
In spirit and voice
Smiling to the sun
Smiling quickly to others
With a twinkle in your eyes
As you focus them on me
You give your time
And unwavering love
To a family that adores you
You share a life with me
From beginning to the end.
I thank you, God
For blessing me
With the man inside the man.

Who Knew

Was I supposed to know
There would be days of tears
Held tightly inside
Until they broke free
Flowing uncontrollably
Down my face
Wet cheeks, salty taste
As they cover my lips
And continue down my neck.

I wipe my eyes,
My cheeks, my lips
My neck
Check the mirror
For signs of fear, worry, confusion
Nothing shows
I leave and join the world
Once more.

Front Window

In these early morning hours
When the day is barely new
I sit and write these poems
And my thoughts are all on you
I can't express in words
There isn't enough time
I count my many blessings
And cherish that they're mine
For I know there'll come a day
When life will close a curtain
But this window that I glance out
Is of immense beauty
I am certain.

I never imagined this course
That the future, our future
Would lead us down this road
Of uncertainty,
Of fear and anxiety
Never knowing, "what next?"
Always on edge,
Alert,
Stressed about everything
And nothing
Complications arise at a moment's
notice
Leaving me tired,
Afraid, drained
And ignorant.

I feel bad
Or is it anger?
Mixed emotions
Fill my mind.
I can't continue
To enable you
Make choices for you
Resenting myself
Or this disease
And what it does
To the one I love.

The blinds that cover
Your eyes
Slowly dropping
Lowering
Like the shield
Covering your thoughts
Guarding you and
Closing me out
As I watch
Knowing it's another
View
Of Alzheimer's.

I can't tell the difference
Anymore.
Is this the process of our life
Or is it the progression of the disease?
Where are all those answers
To all my endless questions.
Support, advocacy, terms newly learned
Are they part of the process
Or are they a requirement
For the progression?
I can't tell.

What is Growing Old Together?

It's working outside
Side by side
Disagreeing and compromising
While smiling at each other
It's getting my coffee
Early in the morning
When you don't even drink coffee
It's filling your pillbox for the week
Because it's too confusing for you
It's turning up the monitor during the day
Because you're super cold
And me turning it down at night
To save energy, and we can snuggle
It's checking all the locks at night
Because you know I get scared.
It's taking out the trash, and the
compost,
But trading turns without saying
anything,
It's my radio station in the morning
And it's your when I leave the bedroom
It's watching your favorite music videos
While I've watched them over and over

continued…

Continued from "What is Growing Old Together?"

It's you doing dishes, every day,
So I can enjoy a clean kitchen
To cook in
It's knowing when to hit "pause" during a stressful time
And hit "continue" after apologies and hugs.
It's looking in your closet
And picking out something without stains
Because you can't see them
It's asking your opinion, "these shoes or these"
Because you have great taste
And I just can't decide.
It's valuing your logical mind
And my artistic one
Without any reservations.

"What's on your agenda today?"
You say
I'm going to the library
To listen to a presentation
"What time?"
You say
It starts at 10:00 am
And should end at noon.
"What's on your agenda today?"
You say
I'm going to the library
To listen to a presentation.
"What time?"
You say
It starts at 10:00 am
I will say several times more...

Sometimes I Wonder

Sometimes I wonder
I wonder about you
And I wonder what's
Happening to your brain.
I wonder if this disease
Is making a move.
I wonder, why you?
And why, or what, took place
That we couldn't change.
I wonder about the future
And I wonder how long
Will we have together?
I wonder when you
Will leave me
But
Still be present.
Sometimes, I just wonder.
I wonder about life.

Remembering

You may not remember the little things
Like your glasses are over there
And your drink is outside,
But you remember our favorite song
And how I out-fished you on our
First date.
You may not remember the details
Of that movie you've seen,
But you tell me, that's the good thing
About this disease, you'll just watch it
again.
You remember what bait to use to catch
Salmon, Steelhead,
Albacore, Halibut,
And the highly prized
Bluefin Tuna
and
You still think I'm beautiful
I'll remember that.

This time together
For as long as it is
Cannot be enough for me.
For time is moving forward
So quickly, too quickly
For me
And I'm uncertain about
Most things.
Going forward with you
Means support, comfort, love.
Forward alone
Looks quiet, scary, and lonely.
I will cherish this time
Together
For as long as it is.

Where are you in this illness?
Does every day look different?
Feel different? Sound different?
Does depression cloud the view,
Muffle the sounds, bury pain?
Can you feel the love of your wife?
The joy from your children?
The blessings of grandchildren?
Where are you in this illness?
From my perspective it's
Like watching someone dissolve
Into another world, without
Knowing others want to help,
Without seeing others, as they
Sit by you.

The sounds you make
When you're asleep
Makes me realize
How restless you are
In your head
As you talk
And move your
Arms and legs
Making me aware
That your movements
Can hurt me
So I urgently
Push you awake
Let you know you're
Dreaming
You mumble
And fall back
To that place
in your head
That I don't see.

The changes
So slight
But
Obvious
To me
I,
Having known
You
Forever
See the disease
Slowly
But surely
Taking you
While I
Watch
And
Wait
With you,
Beside
You.

There are so many others
With issues so much more
Challenging
Than my own
And
I thought I could
Handle all the unexpected issues
In my life without help
I can't.
It's been more than
Three years
Our lives have evolved into???
Constant uncertainty.

Feeling a Bit Lost

I'm feeling a little restless
My thoughts are incomplete
My actions leave me wondering
I have an attitude of defeat —
For a purpose and direction
They usually lead my way
But lately that's all changed course
As I begin another day.
I know that I can focus
And lay out some type of plan
To help me see a better day
To see who I really am

What to Do

You are changing
Once again
The cough you have
As you begin
To start
Each day
Or eat
A meal
The endless
Cough
Even I
Can feel
As your
Body
Shakes
And your
Eyes
Tear up
I
don't
Know
What
To
Do.

You can sit for hours
Staring at …?
You can speak
But
Barely more than
A sentence
You smile at me
At your grown children
At your young
Grandchild
But
I see the tears
Just forming
In those
Bluer than the bluest
Skies
Eyes of yours –
You know
And I know
Change is happening
There's no going
Back
We're in this
Together.

Tears form
As I picture you
Memories of the past
You and your twinkling
Sky blue – see through
Eyes
Ready to smile
At any moment
To everyone
An energy of confidence
But not overwhelming
Surrounded you
Tears form
As I picture you
Lying next to me
Alzheimer's Disease
Taking you
As I watch –
Helpless to stop it.

It's overwhelming
This sense of uncertainty –
What am I doing?
What needs to be done?
There are more directions
More choices
More doubt
More worry that I'll
Forget something
Or
Make the wrong choice
Go in too many directions
Leaving both of us
Lost.
And,
You can't help me.

I don't know what
Your pain is from
Or where it is exactly
I only know I hurt
For you
And I haven't any
Cure.
Time is taking you
Away
In every bone and vein
I watch you wince
So quietly
And shift from
Side to back
I cannot help
But wonder when or what
This pain will attack next?

Sense of Hope

My world is changing
Once again
And I'm learning
How to cope
I'm also learning
Different skills
That give me
A sense of hope
That as this disease
Progresses
And your needs will be
More and more
That I can cope
With every change
Just as I did before.

I am hurt, angry and afraid
The twists and turns of
Our lives, each day,
Every day
Keep me awake
Not knowing what to do
What's up ahead
For us, for me
I am so tired
And my body's on alert
For the sounds and
The movements you make
While asleep
They scare me.

Thinking ahead
Should be fun
Thinking ahead
For two
One with Alzheimer's Disease
Is hard
To do
Every day is different
That's the new "normal"
Thinking ahead is
"Dreaming of"
"Wishing for"
The reality is clear
Thinking ahead,
For two,
I shouldn't.
It's hard enough for one.

In The Time of Alzheimer's

Early morning hours
The day is underway
Pull and tie the curtains back
And hot coffee's on the way

The sound of cars are heard, not seen
As the light begins to shine
Each day brings me a sense of hope
As sleep has cleared my mind

This journey that we're traveling towards
Has so many different twists
That I am constantly faced with choices
And have succumbed to making lists

The hope is that I'll soon erase
These doubts and fears I store
That every day we have together
Is one more that we had before.

Being Thankful

Being thankful
Reminding myself
To appreciate
The love
Of others
Of life
Knowing each day
Can change
The outlook
Of tomorrow.
Be Thankful.

Why I'd Throw the Beans!

I am so frustrated
By you
By myself
Every day I wake up
Happy
And then you wake up
And the atmosphere
Changes
And so do I
You find fault
With my actions
You sulk
If I need to go out
And when I come
Back
You're critical
And negative
Of my every good
Intention or comments
Is it the disease
Or your opportunity
To let me think that
When it isn't?

Is this disease winning
Or are you just being mean
I can't tell the difference
And I won't make a scene
To challenge your comments
With a few words of my own
That's not how this works
Not while we're both in this home!
But the damage continues
And I'm feeling the pain
The residuals from words
In this truly horrible game.

Sitting in a quiet place
Where no one else is near
My thoughts are on the day ahead
My plans are not yet clear
For as I sit and ponder
While looking at the trees
With a gentle movement of the wind
I acknowledge my unease
What will this day bring anew
What actions must be taken
What unforeseen adventure waits
Of this I'm not mistaken
So plan a course of action
But plan it as "Swiss cheese"
And know the day ahead is here
Like that branch moving with the breeze.

So many things now make me sad
The times we used to have such fun
Gone
The memories of our early selves
And the adventures we created
Fading
And the days we have ahead of us
Are filled with a routine, not plans
Boring
And my wish is one that only I know
Just to be with you and smile
Hope.

So many tears
Throughout the day
When I ask you about them
You have nothing to say.

It hurts in my heart
To see all your tears
But I try to control feelings
And hide all my fears.

Do these tears have a meaning
Is there another change in the air?
I just want you to know
I will always be here.

Sometimes the words just flow
Like the river when it's full
And I can sit and write for hours
And let my mind just go
But there are times
When I can't think
And nothing changes that
Not even when the urge is strong
It's the energy that I lack.

Yesterday was worrisome
I noticed a change in you
It was all the tears
Throughout the day,
Well that was something new
I don't know what to do.
And will today be different?
At this point I haven't a clue
But will watch as much as possible
It's just something that I do.

Thanksgiving 2020

Michael,
I thank you for this life we share
The good times and the bad
My love for you has only deepened
Although, yes, you still can make me
mad!
Which only goes to show how much
Your love affects me so,
And on this day, where we give thanks
I thought I'd write this
To let you know
For our future is quite uncertain
The past is done and gone
"Together" we will face today
Knowing "together" is where we are
strong.

Looking back
At another time
When I was young
When life was what, fine?
I read the cards
The letters too
Reminds me of
A different you
We've made choices
We've forged ahead
Held our lives together
With love, not thread
We continue on
One day at a time
Looking back and forward
I'm glad you're still mine.

Stuck!

This feeling
This feeling
Of "stuck"
Is quite honestly
"Yuck"
I can't
Go forward
Move ahead
Going back
Is my biggest
Dread
So,
Being stuck
Must end
Now
If only I
Could figure
Out "how"

We have this time
Now,
The present
Let's enjoy moments
Not minutes
Not hours
Moments and memories
For us
Let's enjoy "us"
In these moments
And new memories
Celebrating the
Old ones
As they too will
Become moments.

Changing times
Change of heart
Change of mind
Will it ever stop?
With no directions
No thought or plan
What happens next
With my loving man?
His health determines
Our next move
Each minute by minute
I haven't a clue
But I go with the flow
Let him dictate the course
Not knowing our fate
But trusting the source.
For now.

I hate this disease.
I hate this pandemic.
They're ruining my days
And
I can admit it!

Leaving Stage One?

From point A to point B
Why can't you see
It's you and not me
And we just don't agree
But I think it's a change
The brain's re-arranged
My words, your hearing
A new stage is nearing
But I am not ready
Things have been steady
Has the time come
Are you leaving stage one?
I'm trying to be smart
But it tears at my heart
To be with you and know
A piece of life's flow
Has taken a twist
One that I'll miss
Together — that's what we do
From one point to another I'll be here
with you.

Memory

It doesn't last
Does it?
This compromised memory
In your brain.
It stays and
Poof — it's gone
Only the music
Stays safely inside
Tucked and protected
So you can sing
Knowing all the words and sounds
Keeping your brain
Active and alert
For the present.

Alzheimer's Disease
Is like a slow cancer
Without surgery or
Any cure yet,
Like watching the
Sunset over the ocean
But falling asleep
Before it's gone
And hoping it was
Beautiful.
Alzheimer's Disease
Takes it's time
But you can see it
It's never gone
Until it sets.

Butterfly Bushes

You hurt my feelings
With your words of hate
Of things I cherish
You don't relate
And I must go
To another place
To escape my anger
Not see your face
Take time to thing
Put things away
To refocus my feelings
Just get through today.

In The Meantime

Looking for clarity
Structure
Purpose
Beyond what's visible
Knowing it's
Out there
Somewhere
Waiting for me
To
Notice
And
I will.

How do I choose
These thoughts and feelings
That express so much
Of you,
Of me
And
This Alzheimer's Disease?
There is no right
Or wrong
My words are to
Be shared
And
Maybe some else
Will relate
To one or two lines
And
Maybe these poems
Can reveal some window
Into the life of a spouse
Who loves the one
With the disease.

At the E.R.

I listened to the stories
Of others standing by
I heard the laughter in his voice
And I heard myself ask why?
Is it funny when confusion
Or is memory loss known?
Is the laughter based on ignorance
Or fears that can't be shown?
But it hurts to hear it
All the same
Knowing as I do
That confusion and such memory loss
Are also happening
To you.

The memories we've created
For ourselves and others too
Have brought so many smiles to all
And my credit goes to you.
For you've spent your time
On things that matter
On outdoor adventures
With lots of fishing chatter
And those that know you
Will always smile
As they picture you fishing
As that's been your style.

As the days go by
Each one unique
You're losing weight
You're getting weak
And I'm not sure
What I can do
To change the day
To better help you
So I'll just continue
To be at your side
To watch you dissolve
While my tears I'll hide.

Changing Stages

Just when it seemed
Life's going forward
Our days together
Filled with light
And a special warmth
A change occurs
And the pattern
Or spell,
Is broken
The light is dimmer
There's a chill
Surrounding us.

Closing Thoughts

By Kelley E. Howe Nolan

It's not always easy to love someone, even in the best of times. I'm fortunate enough to be surrounded by people who love me and remind me that life is as good as it is hard.
Asking for help is a strength.
                    Accepting help is a blessing.

Other Published Works

"I Wish She Were Near" — American Poetry Anthology, Ed. John Frost. California: The American Poetry Association. 1984. p264. Print

"Living Love" — Masterpieces of Modern Verse, Ed. John Frost. California: The American Poetry Association. 1985. p57. Print

"If Only"— Masterpieces of Modern Verse, Ed. John Frost. California: The American Poetry Association. 1985. p153. Print

"Two Little Children" — Best New Poets of 1986, Ed. John Frost. California: The American Poetry Association. 1986. p130. Print

"A Roller-Coaster Love" — Hearts on Fire: A Treasury of Poems on Love, Ed. John Frost. California: The American Poetry Association. 1986. p318. Print

"Click" — Heartland Anthology of Poetry, Ed. Will Stratford. California: The Poetry Center Press. 1989. p71. Print

Other Published Works

"My Children --- (Sarah, Jesse, Matthew)" — The National Poetry Anthology1989 Edition, New York Poetry Anthology, Inc. 1989. p45. Print

"Click" — The Write Stuff, College of the Redwoods, Del Norte. October 1989. p12. Print

"I Wish We Could Share This" — The Write Stuff, College of the Redwoods, Del Norte. October 1989. p12. Print

"Unkind Memories" — The Write Stuff, College of the Redwoods, Del Norte. Spring 1990. p17. Print

"Maybe We're Equals" — The Write Stuff, College of the Redwoods, Del Norte. Spring 1990. p17. Print

"Her Day" — The Write Stuff, College of the Redwoods, Del Norte. Fall 1990. p12. Print

"Trees and Spring" — The Write Stuff, College of the Redwoods, Del Norte. Fall 1990. p12. Print

About the Author

Kelley and her husband reside in Northern California, where the redwoods meet the sea.

Made in the USA
Columbia, SC
24 September 2021

45488568R00048